THE DREAMER

KAREN HOL

Karen Hol

TO GOD BE THE GLORY

Acknowledgments

To my wonderful husband, Richard, who supports my art and encourages me along my journey. His patience in dealing with my challenges with computers, time spent in publishing this book and his appreciation of the arts is an encouragement and blessing to me.

To my beautiful children, my daughter Renee and her husband John Chertudi, my grandchildren, Vanessa, Faith, and great grandchildren Elizabeth and Ryan. My son Jason, his wife Sarah and their lovely children, Ezme and Cyrus. "The beauty and joy you bring to my life inspires me."

To my wonderful parents, the late Donald and Katherine Ivarsen, who encouraged me to pursue my passion in art. To my kind and embracing second parents, the late Ryk & Willemina Hol.

To Sara Bonacum for the many hours she spent editing my original manuscript and for encouraging me along this journey.

To my best friend, the late Jill Austin of Master Potter Ministries, who taught me that being a teacher of the Word of God can be a challenging, yet fulfilling calling. Thank you, Jill, for your friendship.

To my artist friend, the late Marlo Fyfe Sass, for teaching me that not all paintings are the same and for helping me see art in those early years.

Thank you, Marjean Peters for your encouragement and patience editing this book of poetry. Your gifts and talents inspire me to go on with my passion.

Karen Hol – Artist

The dynamic and colorful world of Karen Hol lies nestled in the northeastern Washington mountains in a rugged log cabin during the early years inspired her paintings and writings.

Majestic mountains covered with dense forests and green meadows reflect nature's beauty with an explosion of colors in each season that inspired the artist. Winter preparations include food to can and firewood to gather while the warmth of the wood cook-stove removes the sharp bite of the cold snowy winter. This world stands in sharp contrast to the world of tract homes, supermarkets, and life in the fast lane. Today, Karen's world is filled with life, brilliant color, and creative writing.

This prolific artist paints in strong pure color that demands attention in its simplicity and demonstrates the presence of God in her world. The front cover of this book represents one of Karen's many paintings and the rear cover offer the reader a view of her art studio. While her early years of creative art focused on drawing and painting, she has expanded her expression with the power of words through poetry and deep reflection.

A few words from the artist regarding her drawings and paintings, some of which can be found at: www.karenhol.com:

When I paint, I paint
as a dancer.
A dancer of ideas.
When I paint, I am the dancer,
I dance in color.

I hear music throughout
my paintings.

I feel like a blind
person making my way through
a room—looking for
the color of the symphony
I hear in my drawing.

Born to Fly

I always use the media of oil and acrylic paints to escape into the world of art and creativity. Born in the Pacific Northwest, where the fresh air invigorates me and the color leaves me breathless, I present a new way to look at the world through color, line and, poetry. Self-taught and always launching into new statements of old subjects, I bring you along on my journey into the heavens.

I paint with my emotions and heart while I follow the Creator within. My bold, yet gentle work flows peacefully, yet strong.

I paint slowly so the colors tell me the way to go. Many of my paintings paint themselves while I sit quietly alongside and listen. Color, lines and words speak to me.

I paint in simple line form that captures the viewers' heart and soul.

I love nature and spend many hours in the woods to listen, absorb, and later to paint and write.

Silence speaks to me and I paint the silence and peace around me. The Creator of life teaches and befriends me.

The world rushes past my studio window and I remain inside, warm and absorbed in line, color and the power of words!

Color becomes music and I enjoy its daily symphony in my work.

Dedication

I dedication my first book of poetry to the God of Creation. My heavenly Father and friend. You gave me the talent to show the world your creative hand. You are my Lord and Savior.

Papa, Come Dance with Me

I went into Papa's room and said, "Papa come dance with me." Papa said "yes." He took my tiny hand into his own tiny hand. We both held teddy bears and we danced and we danced. Soon I grew into a young girl with a wide hoop dress and we twirled, and we twirled. Then I became an elegant dancer dancing around Papa and he laughed. Soon He took my hand and He walked me down the aisle and we threw bouquets. We danced long into the starry night and Milky Way. My long and elegant evening dress swept along as we waltzed around and around. Later we danced in the clouds. I wore a halo and He wore a crown. "Thank you, Papa, for the dance."

HE GAVE ME THIS BOOK BY HIS HAND AND NOW I GIVE IT BACK TO HIM BY MY HAND. MAY THE GLORY BE ALL HIS.

TABLE OF CONTENTS

Introduction

Poems

The Early Years

I arrived in 1944, a baby-boomer, an all-American. I love America. When I look at other countries, I feel proud and blessed that God chose America for my home, a nation under God, indivisible, with freedom and justice for all.

I also feel grateful that God chose this time in history to bring me into the world. I realize He did not design me with the ability to survive pioneer life in a covered wagon nor to endure the industrial revolution. This present time with washing machines, cars, computers and airplanes suits me much better. Prior to 1944 the pursuit of art came only for the wealthy. I imagine life during the industrial revolution reduced to survival, rather than a promotion of my destiny for wholehearted, passionate pursuit of art, poetry and writing.

My privileged childhood filled with play in a family who loved nature and fun. From a very early age I played baseball, roller skated, and climbed trees. Not a frilly lace girl, I enjoyed the life of a tom-boy who loved anything to do with nature and the outdoors. My parents found it hard to get me inside for any reason. I always found another baseball game to play, a river to swim, or a kite to fly. My loving parents gave me a lot of free time. Not driven toward high achievement nor college educated, they never pushed the academic world upon me. I grew up as a free spirit to explore outdoor wonders.

My father took me on fishing trips and I remember them all. We fished the mountain streams on Saturdays, and I think those early years cultivated the divine gift and passion for art that flowed through my veins. Most kids think of Saturday chores, but I think of Saturday fishing. I remember the hours I sat on a big rock in the middle of a babbling brook as my father fished. I feel so blest for all those young years when I observed and heard nature, the nuances of the stream, the birds, and the smells of the forest.

When I began my art endeavors I, of course, drew the forests I knew so well, the streams, the mountains, and the trees. While other parents whisked their children off to play competitive sports, I sat alone on a sunny rock and observed God's creation.

My love for God formed in those early years. I knew Him in His creation and I knew He knew me. I felt no fear of being alone on my sunny rock, but rather I felt enchantment, endearment, and peace. My earthly father gave me a wonderful gift when he surrounded me with God's creation. I always thank God for those early years spent in the silence of the forest. Even to this day, I go by myself to a mountain stream and recall all those hours alone with my Creator. I especially love to go out into nature and compose poetry by a quiet stream.

When my parents enrolled me in elementary school, I found myself in a foreign environment. I felt uncomfortable with people, books, lessons, and tests. My comfort remained by mountain streams and in God's creation for hours. I daydreamed in class of mountains, crisp cool streams, and all my forest friends. An artist at heart and not a scholar, books and lessons bored me. When it came to reading, writing, and arithmetic, I could care less. I now realize that educators geared their teaching style for left brain people and I operated from the right. Therefore, the teaching style opposed my God-given design and I fell through the cracks of education. How truly unfortunate that educators don't gear the curriculum or teaching styles for right brain people or toward the passions inside a right brain student. Those gifted in the arts look stupid to the rest of the world. We struggle with academic rhetoric and many drop out of school because of this conflict. I followed expectations, but I hated school and the way they taught. I only excelled in two classes, art and physical education. I never got an "A" in any class and my grades remained only average. College held no attraction for me because I felt unqualified. Later I realized my smarts found expression in the arts on paper and on canvas.

These early judgements, which I placed on myself, set up a lot of barriers for me to overcome. When I finally went to college, in my early thirties, I majored in art and English. As a child, I learned to listen and observe nature by mountain streams and I carried that aptitude into adulthood. My shy and quiet demeanor and desire to listen rather than speak made people think of me as stuck-up. In a group situation, I felt more comfortable as a follower than a leader. I cared very little how other people saw me and felt no need to impress them with exceptional grades. I felt content with a "C" average. My parents applauded me for "C" grades and never pushed me for "A's". How I appreciated their support and encouragement over the years. They saw my passions in art and sports and never put me down because I enjoyed these challenges. They never talked to me about college or high paying jobs. Not rowdy, rude, or out of line in any class or situation, I contented myself to live a quiet life and create from the inside world of art.

God gave me the right parents for my sensitive personality. I remember when I passed my driver's test at nineteen years old. That summer, out of boredom, I decided to read the drivers manual and take the test. The world's pressure for things never affected me. My interest to buy a water ski boat exceeded any interest to buy a car. I just borrowed my father's old pink Plymouth to get the boat to the lake. I never fit the classic image of a child. I thought differently than others and I cared less what other people thought of me. I feel the same way today. I just need to cooperate with how God created me and not try to pattern myself after someone else. The arts always challenged, motivated, and captivated my interest. I feel so glad I followed my heart and passions in life and not ideas put there by other people. I always knew God destined me for art and I feel fortunate that He equipped me to follow those dreams and passions.

My World

Most of you never met me personally or walked into my art studio. You do not know my favorite colors or which foods I like to eat. You probably wonder if I create long into the starry night or if I am a day person and create in the daylight hours. You might wonder if I am a little bizarre, like some artists of the past.

I composed a few questions and answers to give a little peek into my world.

- Where were you born and when?
    - I entered this world September 26, 1944 in Tacoma, Washington. I am an American with stubborn Norwegian blood in my veins. My grandparents came from Oslo, Norway.

- Who were your parents and what were they like?
    - My parents were Donald Ivarsen and Katherine (Katie) Jean Ivarsen (Miller). Both my parents were born and raised in Tacoma, Washington. My father was Norwegian, and my mother was Austrian/Norwegian. Both my parents were soft spoken and engaging.
    - My father and grandfather were avid fishermen. I fished as a child on Mount Rainier streams and lakes with my father.

- Did you do art as a child?
    - Yes. I remember drawing in grade school. I also took a drawing class in 9th grade and loved it. I remember I bought a paint-by-number set of dogs. I loved doing that painting and it opened the world of painting before my eyes. I continued to take art classes through High School and later in College. I loved everything about the world of art and I became passionate to express myself In line and color. I soon recognized this passion as my destiny to express myself through drawing, painting, and later photography and writing. The more art I did, the more I wanted to do.

- Did either of your parents or relatives do art?
    - Neither of my parents did any kind of art. My Aunt Jo did watercolor paintings, my only relative who did art. I remember her tiny apartment with small paintings everywhere. I used to visit Aunt Jo every week after swimming lessons. I enjoyed her wonderful world of watercolor paintings. She passed away when I was twelve years old and I inherited several of her paintings. I saw her as my hero and wanted to emulate her.

- What were you like as a child?
    - I felt extremely shy and introverted as a child. My brother Ray was four years older and a big tease. I think his teasing caused me to withdraw and feel shy because he joked about everything and usually at my expense. As a tomboy, I loved the outdoors and to play baseball, or climb trees. I hated to play with dolls or hang around the girls who played house.

- Did you enjoy school?
    - I daydreamed in school, always looked out the window, longed for recess and impatiently waited to go outside. Reading and grammar bored me. I struggled with school, hated tests and went into a brain freeze when the teacher passed out the test. I grew up thinking I was stupid because I struggled in school. I only excelled in art and physical education and did not go on to college until almost thirty years old. I hated school but loved art.

- Did you know you would become an artist someday?
    - I did not know I would be an artist until I started drawing daily while living in San Francisco. I think I realized I wanted to be a full-time artist at that time. When I married, I fulfilled my dream to become an artist. You can see my art work at www.karenhol.com

THE DREAMER

BY KAREN HOL

THE DREAMER

You are the dreamer!

The dream is unknown
until you dream it,
walk it,
live it!

The dreams are all inside you!

Let your spirit awake
to the dreamer.

You will need to
listen,
ponder,
and accept
how God made you.

God is a dreamer too!

Listen,
ponder,
and accept yourself,
then follow your dreams!

We all dream because God gave that gift to everyone without limit. Dreams come naturally to children before adulthood chases them away. Visions of possibilities change us, stretch us and many times fulfill us. It all depends on how we engage our dreams. Will we take the risk to step out into the vast unknown to achieve them? My desire to live in San Francisco, Hawaii, and later in Aspen, Colorado became a reality only because I planned and followed those dreams. I love to envision plans that are birthed in dreams, but to live them excites me even more. Because not all ideas turn out the way we plan, I found it best to dream up a plan "b" if plan "a" falls through. A job interview to teach water skiing in upstate New York raised my hopes, but when circumstances beyond my control changed that plan, I dreamed again. We must not let the death of one dream crush our imagination. When we enter the final years of our journey here on earth, it becomes even more critical to keep our hopes alive. I dream of heaven which genuinely exhilarates me. I plan to continue writing and painting when I get there. I hear it contains new and assorted colors, so I expect to compose many paintings with them. I also look forward to all the new art venues in heaven. My soul needs to dream because dreams invigorate me and keep me alive.

SO, DREAM BIG

I took a painting class once,
but I left the class
on the second or third evening
never to return.

I took a class on poetry
and never finished it.

"How can someone teach me
how to paint or write?" I said.

"Won't I be taught how they paint
and they write,
or how someone taught them?"

"No," I said to myself,
"I will paint
and I will write
and the way I paint and write
will come forth from who I am,
what I see, and how I feel."

No one can teach me who I am,
except me.

"By painting one becomes a painter" Vincent van Gogh

This poem gives direction to my art. I feel fiercely independent when it comes to art and how to express it. My artist friend went to the university and lost her style. They taught it out of her because the way we think is the way we paint. They taught her to think differently about art and she began to paint like them. It amazes me that teachers wield so much power. I feel very glad a university education never afforded itself to me. I learned art on my own. I looked through art books and learned to see art. Little by little I formed my conclusions about art and how to do it. Others never took away or influenced my style. We need to guard our style. Our passions must stay our passions to the end. We must remain true to ourselves to our last breath.

BELIEVE IN YOURSELF

You must
believe in yourself.

To stand alone
never comes easily.

No one ever said
it would be.

Others might see
and believe,
but most will not.

It only matters
that you see
and believe
in yourself.

An artist in any field of expression understands what it means to believe in yourself. To stand alone and believe takes a lot of inner tenacity. Talent often goes unrecognized but needs expression with or without recognition. I plod along because I believe in the way I do my art and that alone matters to me. I paint for an audience of one. I do art because the Creator gave me the gift of artistic expression. Art drives me from the inside. When I stop the process, something inside of me stops. I cannot continue through life without painting or writing. Some artists never receive recognition in their lifetime, many never receive much praise or money for their artwork. Van Gogh lived a lifetime without recognition. Now his paintings sell in the million-dollar range. Go figure. Every artist lives with this reality and must choose to ignore it. We write because of our passion to write. Our passion and delight sources itself in art. With or without accolades, we produce art.

A POET

A poet to me
captures a second
and freezes it into a sentence
that oozes with emotion and life.

A second suspended between
spoken and unspoken words.

A second says it all
and leaves nothing out.

A sentence in a word,
a novel in a sentence.

Poets do it
like no others.

Buckshot riders
on a stagecoach of life.

Poets do it
like no others.

Creative people mesmerize us with their God-directed talents. The Creator dazzles us with His paint brush on autumn and we possess that same gift with our paint brush on canvas. God paints big, very big, but then He is God. A poet's unique gift says myriads of things in a single sentence. They paint a landscape with their words. They paint history and its people in living color. They awaken our soul to the unspoken words in a sentence and the unseen colors in a painting. Poets dance to their own music. All that music within their spirit draws us into their muse like buckshot riders on the stagecoach of life. I heard it said, "Art stirs us, but words pierce us. "Words do pierce our souls and encourage or defeat us. The poet knows all too well about the power of words. I also heard it said, "The pen is mightier than the sword." Both statements resonate deep within my spirit as I write poetry and paint.

DIVINE GIFTS

Poems come to me,
a gift
divinely given.

I do not seek them,
they seek me.

I do not wait for them,
they wait for me.

I do not own them,
they own me.

They are God's gift to me
divinely given.

I believe in dreams and I also believe in the Creator who sends divine ideas and dreams. If I take credit for my poems and paintings, then Creator, who gave them to me, receives no credit. I feel truly grateful for the gift of art inside me. Papa God enables the hand of the sculptor, as well as the surgeon's hand. If we take credit, we miss the joyous delight to praise and glorify Him for our talents and gifts. I believe poems wait for me to write them. I only must listen for His voice in my head or heart. The gift lives within and never goes away day or night. We do not own this gift, but it avails itself to share in whatever way we choose. I hope you share your God-imparted gift with the world. The first artist created us, and His canvas stretched across the universe. He also wrote one book—the Bible. He shared and so must we.

Each person's creative gift and expression of that gift differs from mine. No two artists paint or write music in the same way. God created each of us unique. Even two painters who paint the same subject see and paint it differently. To compare ourselves with others kills creativity. We do not have to express ourselves like someone else. The artists who came before us will influence us, but no one expresses their talent in the same way. Every style and every expression of art holds validity. Many people will never identify with my art or my poem style. I accept that. I also know many people accept my artwork. Regardless, I write and paint freely. I express myself with no anchor of public opinion.

A BOOK

Someone I knew
for a brief time
suffered a heart attack
and graduated to heaven.

Her husband was shocked
at all the sympathy cards
he received.

I told my husband
"Don't expect many
cards for me."

My husband replied
"She received many cards,
but your books live on."

That put everything
into perspective for me.

Eternity will write
our worth and grant rewards
when our journey ends
and a new book written.

I consider friendships precious. Though few, their worth glows like gold in my treasure box. Many of my artist friends understand the price an artist pays for the gift of art. We work hard at our gifting to perfect it over the years. When my husband said, "She receives many sympathy cards, but books live on," he gave me such honor that I cried inside. He sees my dedication and hard work over the years and it truly blessed me that he saw the end reward. I chose my God-given destiny over multiple relationships. As artists, we cannot sustain both. It takes many hours of quiet time in the art studio to express those God-inspired passions. Many artists, like myself, chose destiny instead of mingling with the crowd. This quiet and shy child developed into an artist and writer slowly over the years. When I married, I embraced the opportunity to spend long hours in pursuit of my God-given talent. I recognize that God truly blessed me with a husband who loves and supports my passions.

A QUIET DAY IN THE STUDIO

Many
quiet days
in my art studio.

Delightful days,
listening days,
silent days.

Only the sound of wind
and the bending of trees
outside the large studio window.

I watch the
clouds roll by
as I create.

The music comes from within
because silence speaks to me,
always.

To work in my art studio feels like no other experience in life. I enjoy every silent hour. I hear the world outside, but my own world of color, line, and canvas hold me passionately captive. The artist within loves to write about my painting journey daily. Sometimes no words come to explain the challenge and excitement to complete a poem or a painting in the studio. No other challenge compares to a white canvas or a blank sheet of paper. The adventure and excitement to watch a painting emerge out of empty space seems unbelievable. The hours feel like minutes when I express my soul on canvas. The poem and the painting mirror my internal world in the same the way that mountain streams reflected my childhood. In my studio, I like quietness to focus on my inner thoughts and ideas. I never seem to run out of innovative ideas. That becomes problematic when I end up with too many unfinished projects. This seems a common problem for other creative people I meet. To finish each project takes a lot of inner tenacity, much like scaling the highest ridge on a mountain.

Artists need time and the passion to follow their dreams. We need to guard our time and not allow other things to steal it. God bless you as you follow your dreams.

SENSITIVITY

We know sensitivity,
but the world shuts it down inside us.

Don't cry.
Don't laugh too loud.
Don't be a girl.
Don't be so sensitive.

Sensitivity defines us and
who we become
if we don't shut down.

Sensitivity wakes us up and
puts us to sleep,
if we don't shut down.

Sensitivity is the child within!

I stopped when I came across the word, "sensitivity" in an article I read a few years ago. The word felt electric with a life of its own. At that moment, I knew a poem, a darn good poem, begged for expression. It only took a few minutes to write it. The word waited for me to ponder it and follow the magic. It wrote itself. Like the statue within the marble, it only needed an artist to chisel it out of the stone. God created each of us with sensitivity to follow our own special destiny. But we need to guard our hearts and minds to keep that sensitive small child alive inside us. We also need to allow ourselves the freedom to express our own colors and the music that sings and dances within. Never let anyone take away or shut down the gift within.

KID THINGS

Kids are grand,
they haven't learned
how to be adults yet.

So, they just do kid things.

I learned how
to be an adult once.

I wrote it down
on a piece of lined paper
and
I accidentally
left it in my back pocket.

It went through
a double wash
and I could not read it.

So,
I went back
to being a kid.

It was less of a hassle!

I keep the kid inside me alive through spontaneity and curiosity. To learn about painting, poetry, art, music, nature, and complex landscapes, never ends for a curious person. Creative ideas flow from curious minds. I look for friends who also enjoy spontaneity and fun. I enjoy the company of other free-spirited artists who challenge and inspire me to write and paint. Over the last seventy years I discovered something special and intriguing about other artists. I enjoy the hours and days I spend with artist friends. I especially enjoy those who think way outside the box.

The world teaches us how to act like adults. We learn it well and it stifles the creative child within. Some people call art useless and a waste of time. They rather play games on a computer for hours and hours. I prefer to use my time for challenging creations that last. Everyone must make their own choice on how to use their time on this earth.

THE GOD OF THUNDER

In my house
everyone sleeps
except me.

The God of thunder came to visit tonight.
He lit up the sky with a thousand volts of light.

While the city slumbered,
the God of Heaven thundered.

He calls himself,
"The Great I Am."

Anyone who hurls thunder bolts
across the sky definitely
deserves the name,
"The Great I Am."

I watched in wonder as
He wrote His name
in lightning bolts.

No one does lightening
like
"The Great I Am"
does lightening.

No one!

He is the God of Thunder.
He is the Creator of Life.

He entertained me for hours
and I finally went to bed at three a.m.

In forty-one years of marriage, I now enjoy an art studio with an unobstructed view of the sky. It rises above a two-car garage and a very large window makes me feel like I live in the sky. Every storm I witness thrills me! In thunderstorms, it is just me, God, and the sky. I love to watch the snow and the rain, but thunder remains my all-time favorite.

The God of the Bible, Creator of our universe, befriended me at a very early age. I think I invited Him into my heart and life at about seven years old. I always loved to read the Bible and go to church. When still a child, I met Him as my Savior, but now I know Him as my Lord, which means I include Him in everything I do, both large and small. I pray for His guidance in everything. I rather do life His way than my way. I cannot see around the corner or what lies ahead, so I don't want to risk a decision I might regret for years.

HOUSE ON THE EDGE OF TOWN

What would I do
without country?

We live here
on the edge of town
but
what would I do
without country?

City living is too confining
and phony for my longing
country heart.

I can smell the country
from my art studio window.

The long shadows of summer
draw me outside to listen
to the sounds of country.

I was born in the city
but I have a country heart.

The country has freedoms
the city dwellers will never
understand or embrace.

I will live on the edge of town
but always embrace the country
inside my heart.

Although born in the city, I do not relate to it as I relate to the country. The country reflects my nature and my quiet observance mirrors the country. I easily spend many hours in nature, where I feel right at home, while I draw streams and woods. I still carry fond childhood memories of when we rose at the crack of dawn, packed a large sack lunch and traveled to my father's favorite mountain stream to fish for the entire day. We always traveled a distance to find the best fishing and ventured into the vast wilderness over fallen trees and dense underbrush to finally arrive at our quiet destination. My father left me on a large rock in the sun and then he fished up and down the stream for the entire day. The artist inside this young heart enjoyed every moment of silence. I listened to nature move around my rock castle. The birds serenaded me by the hour. I never felt afraid in nature because my loving father checked back on my rock castle hourly. I think my love for nature and art formed in those early childhood years on my rock by the cold mountain waters. Born in the awesome state of Washington beneath the grandeur of Mount Rainer, the God of Creation gave me a wonderful childhood.

Later in my teens, my parents owned a home in town, but we also enjoyed a lake home. Perhaps nature got into my blood there. All those days and summer evenings on the lake created an indwelling love for nature like my early years on the mountain streams.

Autumn threw color
at my window, this morning.

Gold,
burnt amber,
shimmering green.

It said, "Come play with me!

WATCH ME DANCE FROM TREE TO TREE!"

So...
I went out and danced with autumn
and...

"AUTUMN BECAME ME!"

My husband dreamed of building a log house. When he, our daughter Renee, and our son Jason moved to our twenty-two acres of land in Eastern Washington in 1985, that dream became reality. We purchased the land nine years prior for $15,000 and spent every vacation working to improve the homestead. The property included a small two-room log house built in the early 1900's with no foundation. Many pieces of horse drawn equipment lay everywhere, obviously a settler's homestead. We never knew who fenced the land, tilled the soil, or carried water from the nearby creek. A large deteriorating barn stood tall on the land but eventually collapsed, probably from too much winter snow build-up. We assumed the several smaller log structures on the property housed other animals. We worked many years before we moved onto the property. Prior to our move we built a garage/shop, which we used for a school room after we lived there. I home schooled our two children for several years. I always dreamt of cultivating an acre garden full of fruits and vegetables. This beautiful place allowed that dream to come true. One summer vacation my husband put up a very tall fence around the acre garden. He also built a safe play area with a tall log tree-house for the children while we built the 2,200-square foot log home.

When we lived in the two-room log house, I penned this poem about dancing with autumn. One cold October morning I opened the bedroom curtains and there, on the top of the hill that overlooked the cabin, a brightly colored autumn tree smiled down on me. I felt like the lone tree threw color at me from afar. That moment remains fixed in my memory. The colors shouted from the hillside and I wrote the poem within minutes. I felt like the colors invited me to come outside and dance in the early morning sun. I am not a dancer, so instead, I picked up my pen and danced with the autumn colors on paper.

WINTER HAS COME

Soft footprints appear
in the snow
outside my studio window.

Winter swirls in
and oh, how I love winter.

I blaze with color inside.

Winter paints outside,
I paint inside.

Laughter within and without!

Winter knows my
heart,
mind,
soul!

She understands
the painter within!

She paints outside,
I paint inside.

Winter swirls in at last!

I love the fall and winter seasons best. Something about the cold seasons ignites the fires of creativity inside me. I love winter in my art studio. The day ends early and the night goes on forever as winter settles over the land. The magic of snow inspires my soul and I love to sit at my studio window and watch it fall for hours. I wrote many poems while I watched the snow come down. The autumn colors and the magic of the snow write many poems across my heart. I just draw them out from within. Since I spend many hours alone in silence when I create, I like to take a snow break and walk in the whipped cream powder. Many hours of my life fill with walks in nature while I listen to its sounds. Later I paint from that silent place within. After we built our log house and lived on the land, I remember the many hours I walked and prayed while the snow fell around me. God sends His special gift of silence to the world through the quietness of snow.

TO STAY CREATIVE

To stay creative
takes an iron will,
hard hat and
steel boots!

It comes hard,
very hard.

Everything pulls us away with
distractions by the boxcar load.

We must stay focused,
very focused.

Everyone creates differently.

Some paint late,
some paint early,
and some don't paint at all.

Some possess talent and bury it,
others build cities.

To stay creative
takes an iron will,
hard hat,
steel boots.

This poem holds a special place in my heart. I find it truly difficult to follow my artistic destiny. Everyone else seems to play it safe. To stay creative means we keep our passion alive and give expression to the passions inside. Our busy world of performance, recognition, and money makes it very difficult to remain focused and passionate. Most artists never achieve either of these. Artists create for the love of art, not for the love of money. In our busy world, computers and television rob people's minds of creative pursuits. I see hours of mindless entertainment wasted on talented children of God. I refuse to let these time-thieves steal my talent. I seldom watch television. Over the years I realized that I must "guard my time" if I want to create a legacy. I leave behind a repertoire of art as my greatest contribution to future generations.

My passion to draw and paint came at an early age. Although I never became the best artist in my art classes in junior high and high school, I never gave up my passion to draw and paint. When I traveled to San Francisco, Hawaii, and Aspen, Colorado, I drew in each location. When I married at thirty-one, I pursued my passions even more meaningfully because of my generous and supportive husband. The first year of our marriage the Holy Spirit impressed on my heart to number both my drawings and paintings. I gave titles, dates, and information about each piece of art work. It took long hours to create a volume of my work. Staying creative remained a challenge with the addition of two children, home school, and building our large log house. We also planted, continuously maintained, and harvested an acre of garden. In our thirties, my husband and I shared the dream to build that log home and live on the land. We fulfilled that dream.

ANOTHER DAY WELL DONE

Another day up in song,
another day well sung.

The evening shadows fall
over tired eyes.

A day of memories
gone by.

A day of texture,
line,
words.

A day of boldness,
a day of brightness
swallowed up in shadows
of the setting sun.

Another day well done.

My art days never stay the same. With many different passions in the arts, days flow in various pursuits of expression. I love to draw in bold lines and paint in bold colors. Poetry spins continually through my head and onto paper. I also love photography and writing books on assorted topics. I see myself as a kaleidoscope person. My personal artistic passions hold excitement day after day. I never experience writer's block because when one art expression grows cold another expression burns hot and I follow it. Boredom never finds me.

CHRISTMAS ON THE PORCH

Christmas is long gone
but you would never know it
at my girlfriend's house.

The box of Christmas lights
only made it to the porch.

The lights still twinkle
as the spring rains
pour through the rain gutters.

No one seems to care
or notice that Christmas
is still happening
on this porch.

How long will this box stay
unnoticed on the porch?

Probably until the summer heat
brings someone outside
for the sunshine

and then perhaps the box will
be carried to the attic
for its proper burial until
Christmas celebrations
bring it out again.

I stepped outside on this spring afternoon to wait while my girlfriend Jerry changed for our outing in the park. Then I spotted the Christmas box. . . and the poem began, in this quiet neighborhood I stood in silence to listen to the rain pour through the gutters. The Christmas lights on top of the open box seemed to sing in the rain. The rain wrote this poem while it stared at me that afternoon. I seemed to hear shouts of glee as they unwrapped presents in the background of this silent day. Christmas, though long over for the rest of us, remained for this house, and for this porch. Christmas lived on and no one in the busy house minded. I still see myself on that spring afternoon so long ago. A poem etched it forever in my mind. I like to write poetry because it freeze-frames anything and locks it into a poem or story.

THE RICH MAN AND THE POOR MAN

The rich man keeps buying
what the poor man
can never own.

He builds bigger barns
and bigger houses
to hold his treasures.

The poor man
only has the treasures
in his heart.

The treasures
the rich man
can never own.

They may both
go to heaven.

The rich man poor
and the poor man rich.

This poem came one day while I drove to swim class. I thought about how we take nothing to heaven, not even a penny, but we take what we become into the spirit realm. If we spend our time here on earth to serve others and give our time and money for heavenly purposes, we lay up treasures in Heaven and become rich in spirit. I see so many materially wealthy people who do not talk about God or spend time with Him in His word. They remain penniless in God's eyes. Their earthly possessions do not impress the God of Creation and they must leave their possessions behind for someone else. They depart in spirit to heaven, but many arrive penniless in their spirit man. They used their God-given talents to glorify themselves instead of to give God the glory. I wonder what God will say to them when they reach heaven?

CAFÉ LAROSE

The artists come here,
painters of the universe.

Dreamers with big dreams!

Some see their dreams fly,
others die with the dreams still inside.

No one knows who will fly
and who will die.

No one talks about flying or dying.

The artists only talk about their dreams
and visions.

Inside.

The idea for café La Rose came from a photograph I spotted in a magazine. I tore it out and painted it without the old patron sitting at the table. Artistic minds meet at Café La Rose to discuss ideas and visions in each artist's mind. My best friend Marlo and I spent many hours in coffee shops and in our studios to discuss our plans for the next paintings. We inspired each other with grandiose ideas. I think artists got together in cafés, in each other's studios, or gathering places for centuries. I imagine Van Gogh and his fellow artist friends talking for hours about their art and the art of other artists.

VINCENT VAN GOGH

Van Gogh knew
and painted
what he knew
about life and sorrow.

Sensitive,
alive,
knowing.

He expressed it all
in deep passionate colors
squeezed from his
inner soul.

Poems written
in line and bold color.

Poems from within
no one could hear yet.

No one could understand
yet.

He sang alone,
he sang in death.

He expressed it all
in color.

I admire the works of many artists before me, but as a painter, I identify with Vincent van Gogh. Not because I married a Dutch man or that my last name reveals Dutch ancestry, but because Vincent devoted himself to painting and painted a large volume of work during his lifetime. He made the statement, "By painting one becomes a painter," and I believe in this truth. Not art school but painting makes us painters. Vincent did not fit into the art of his day and I find the same applies to me. I do not bother to go to gallery shows because I cannot identify with the art displayed today. True artists rarely fit into the mainstream of art. Art moves in self-expressed passion of what we think, feel, and believe.

THE DANCER OF IDEAS

The ideas come. . .
sometimes slowly,
sometimes rapidly.

They do not stay long.

They linger for a moment
or two,
sometimes three.

But unless you catch them,
they are gone.

On to the next artist,
painter,
writer.

Unless you catch them
they are gone forever.

Ideas come in rapid succession and vanish just as quickly. Poems come into my head and I quickly write down the title or usually the entire poem. Many times, I hear poems when I drive to work or shop for groceries. At those times, I only pen the title and later write the poem. We never know when a poem decides to impress itself in our mind. I find if I neglect to lock the idea down in written form, it vanishes into thin air. When an idea comes in the middle of the night, I trained myself to turn on a low overhead light and write the idea down. In the morning, I complete it. Once while I drove my car, I heard the same poem again and again in my head. Finally, I pulled over and wrote it down. I find it unusual for poems to repeat themselves over and over. Usually I only get one chance to put it in written form before my active brain skips on to the next thought. The dancer in me wants to waltz on her way and, in a flash, she flies out the window of my brain. I imagine that to catch a butterfly in motion and bring it into our world feels much the same.

MAGICAL NOTES ON A TINY VIOLIN

Hardly anyone lives
in the quiet zone.

Artists live in the quiet zone
alone but
never alone.

They create from within
magical notes
on a tiny violin.

They dance and sing
in the quiet zone
while others sleep.

They catch the wind
and fly overhead
playing magical notes
on a tiny violin.

When I look at this poem I see the tiny statue in my studio of
Fiddler on The Roof. My best friend, Jill Austin of Master Potter
Ministries, brought it back from Israel when she traveled there. It
sits on my studio bookshelf. I think the idea for this poem came
from that tiny statue. In my head, I see images of the fiddler
dance across the rooftops and he reminds me of all the artists I
know. The violin resounds and penetrates my soul. Sometimes it
feels like I play a musical instrument while I paint.

The works of the Romantic Russian painter, Marc Chagall,
inspired the image of the violin player. especially his color plate
27, "Music," and the color plate 38, "The Violinist." I see the
images of his playful paintings in this poem about artists who
play music for the world beneath their gaze.

TREES AND REFLECTION

How can you
or I resist
a sunlit path leading
into a forest?

Doesn't the forest
call your name?

Whispering,
come away
into nature's magical land.

The cool breeze
ripples the tree leaves
like a tiny brook
singing to you,
come away.

The child within
responds in delight
as we leave
the grown-up world behind
and engulf ourselves in
nature's enchanted forest.

Nature will always
call us back
because
we are all tall trees

I grew up a shy and introverted child. I loved nature and in school I daydreamed, stared out the window, and yearned to go outside to draw or run through the trees. I achieved only average grades and waited until my twenties to attend college, never academic, but always artistic, I knew my right brain dominated my thoughts and attitudes. I loved recess. This poem embraces my soul and the love of nature inside me. I am not a city person, but a country girl whose father fished the mountain streams. On Saturdays, we got up very early, packed a large lunch, and headed off to his favorite fishing places. I grew up in Washington State where hundreds of streams and lakes offer many choices. My father and I climbed over heavy underbrush and logs to find the best fishing holes. He left me on a large rock in the middle of the stream and then fished up and down the stream, but checked on me constantly. I remember those sunny days on the huge rock and the many hours I listened to birds and forest sounds. I love to draw trees and nature because it settled inside me as a very young child. Deep in the forest and away from roads or even trails, we never saw anyone when we fished. I remember my father as a great man, whom I plan to see in heaven someday and fish with him once again.

ARISE SPRING! ARISE!

Color blows trumpets
of spring coming alive.

Mornings awake with songs
and winter fades into silence.

Blossoms throw life
into the atmosphere.

The awakening of
a spring morning.

The artist arises
to the color,
music,
the dance,
and the cool air.

Summer will arise
and summersault
into our longing embrace.

The winter will be long forgotten
as we step outside
into the spring air.

Arise spring! Arise!

When spring arrives, I take out my camera and head to my favorite parks and streams to capture the soft colors on the trees and grass. Each season captures the heart of this artist and ignites a passion to capture the soft beauty in pictures. The snow slowly disappears, and the robins return to announce the arrival of spring. Summer, just around the corner, promises to bring the joy of outdoor adventures. Slowly the blossoms on the trees bud into trumpets of color. They arise to sing us a song that intensifies each day. I watch the plants come up through the thawed ground and slowly unfold into bright summer colors. I especially love the vibrant tulips and pansies. As the days become warmer and spring buds appear on the trees, I feel excited about the outdoors after the long winter. Spring holds a special place in my heart because I see new life on aged branches. It reminds me that even though I grow older with each year that passes, I still feel young, joyful, and alive inside. The many forms of art, into which I put myself, also keep me alive inside.

DREAMS AND DREAMERS

Dreams are made
on match book covers,
napkins,
and paper.

They are easy to dream,
long to fulfill.

They are black and white
in the beginning
and full of radiant color and glory
when finished.

Dreams belong to dreamers
willing to risk
and never say die
unless they are truly dead.

Dreams belong to you and me
and anyone willing to dream.

So, dream!

In 1997, I painted two pictures entitled: "The Dreamer" and "Dreams Never Fade." The spark for these paintings came from a book about canyons in America and each painting spoke a poem into me. This happens to me many times. Ideas pop into my mind at unexpected times. When an idea comes to me, I quickly pencil it down on anything available, like napkins or match books. I titled this book "The Dreamer" because I dream. We all dream. Some dreams never become anything but dreams. Many of my ideas for paintings never get off the ground. Others develop into magnificent works of art. Though many of my paintings failed, I keep painting because ideas never fade. They all wait patiently inside me.

YOU HAVE A SONG WORTH SINGING

You have a song
worth singing.

You have a life
worth living.

You have a destiny
waiting.

There will be many opportunities ahead,
keep looking.

Find the song within and
sing it.

Find the poem written
on your heart and
write it.

Find yourself
and then share yourself
with the world.

You have a song
worth singing.

You have a life
worth living.

Find your song! The awesome Creator of the universe put within you a special talent to share with the world. Not everyone writes or paints, but God gave each of us our own special gift. In fact, He gave several talents to each of us. He provides different opportunities to find our special gift, but they take pursuit. I signed up for an art class in the ninth grade and found my love of art in that class. My unique art teacher opened the world of art to me. Ever since that ninth-grade class, I pursued some form of art even through my travels to San Francisco, Hawaii, and Colorado. I only completed a few drawings every year, but I kept the dream alive. After I married, I found more time to pursue my love for drawing, painting, and writing poetry. Value your dream enough to keep it alive and pursue it no matter how small. I never used to consider myself a writer for the simple reason that I could not spell, however, spell check became my best friend. I found my song and I intend to sing it until I graduate to Heaven. I'm confident my journey will continue upstairs with the creative God I serve. Find the song within you and don't let it fade away. Follow my example and keep your dream alive!

THE HEAVENS WILL SING YOUR SONG IN THE NIGHT

If you listen,
really listen,
the heavens will sing songs
in the night.

When the earth is silent
and the wind listens,
you can hear it
far
far away
in the distance.

"You can hear your song."

But you must listen,
really listen,
and
the heavens will sing "your song" in the night!

While I painted "The Heavens Will Sing Your Song in the Night" (painting # P432 done on 2-16-98), I heard this poem within. It means that before we reach heaven, the angels sing about what we accomplish here on earth for the glory of Jesus Christ. "Glory" means to reveal, so we reveal God through His creative power in our lives. He created us to bring glory to the Son of God, and if we follow our destiny, we reveal Him to the world.

Our creative passions draw us to our destiny. Every one of us possess different passions in life. When we follow those passions, we give God glory. Even as a youth I felt passionate about drawing. I took art classes in junior high to pursue that passion. My aunt inspired me because of her love of watercolors. She lived alone, spent most of her time painting, and filled her tiny apartment with her paintings. I visited her every week after swim lessons. Perhaps her inspiration and love of painting encouraged me as a young person to follow my love for drawing, and later painting.

A beautiful broach gave birth to this painting and poem. My wonderful artist friend, Glenda Bakken, gave me a broach of a shooting star one Christmas. When I opened the tiny box, however, I saw the big star at the top and the smaller stars beneath it. That arrangement stuck in my mind, so I did not connect the dots to turn it sideways on my garment. This pin so blessed and inspired me that I did a painting of these stars. When I went to the art meeting, I wore the broach and Glenda remarked, "How novel." I wondered what she meant. Later, I looked again at the broach and noticed the sideways clasp. I turned it and saw a shooting star. But, I felt quite delighted that I painted my own interpretation of these awesome stars.

ONLY ONE BOOK

Papa God
only wrote one book.

He had plenty of time
to write another
but one was sufficient
to explain His all in all.

He is the Ancient of Days,
the Revelator of revelations
and the Wisest of the wise.

He is the Prophet of prophets,
the King of kings
and the Lord of lords.

His book is never outdated
and never totally understood.

How can we understand
a God who makes galaxies,
rainbows, and tornados?

God never expected us
to understand it all
because we are finite
and He is infinite.

He only expected us
to read it.

So, have you read His book?

The Creator of the universe lives with us. I know Him as Papa God, my Heavenly Father. Though introduced to Him as a small child, I came to know Him as Lord of my life in my twenties. Back in the sixties and seventies a spiritual movement gave birth to the Jesus People, hippies who searched for truth and found it in Jesus. As part of that movement I came to know Jesus as my Lord and Savior in 1969. I made him Lord of my life and He remains by my side and my best friend. We both communicate as writers; however, His eternal book never passes away and remains the greatest story ever told. He alone exists as the revealer of revelations and the wisest of the wise. This King of kings created the heavens and the earth. He authored the Bible and reveals truth through parables and stories.

If you desire to meet Him, pray this simple prayer:

"God of this awesome universe, I desire to know You. I need You to forgive my mistakes and sins. I give You my life and my will from this day forward. As I read Your book, please reveal and apply the truth within its stories and parables to me. In Jesus name, I pray this prayer. Amen."

When you read His book, start with Matthew in the New Testament because it provides a great introduction to the person and love of Jesus.

THE PAINTER SELDOM SLEEPS

The painter
seldom sleeps.

Always inside
there is a stirring.

Deep within
a restless turning
of creative energy.

Always seeing beyond
what is seen.

Reaching far above
and touching the unseen.

Always reaching
further than before.

The painter
seldom sleeps.

An artistic person always processes information and seeks innovative ways to express it in their own venues. A restlessness stirs inside their brain to see the unseen. Even through midnight hours the artistic person processes information from the previous day. Excitement and joy rise in the pursuit of the unseen. Many times, in the middle of the night an idea comes to me. I'm compelled to get up and express it on paper before I lose it. My most creative ideas come in daylight but occasionally they come at night. When these creative ideas come, I test the spirit to determine if they are divinely inspired.

How privileged I feel as the recipient of these ideas. I believe the impression to add comments to all my poems came through divine inspiration. I take no credit. I pray consistently throughout the day and the ideas come and I feel extremely blessed. I dream with many daylight visions and I thank the Holy Spirit for this daily gift of insight and inspiration

A TRUE FRIEND

How do you tell
a true friend from
a friend?

Time,
likes,
dislikes,
hearing,
saying.

Walking together
in sun and
in rain.

Listening and
knowing.

True friends
last all seasons and
for all reasons.

True friends stay
when others leave.

That's how you tell
a friend from
a friend.

Friends develop into special and unique paintings. I treasure every one of them. Artists comprise many of my close friends and two best friends wait for me in Heaven. Jill Austin worked as a professional potter and an ordained minister. She managed a group of people who made up her "drama team". Over the years, I traveled with her team in ministry. My other longtime painter and writer friend, Marlo Fyfe (Sass), used an art studio in a warehouse in San Francisco. About ten years ago, I purchased Marlo's best painting of a nude woman, a beautiful piece of art that showed her talent. For forty years we walked together through many joys and sorrows of life. We met in our early twenties and both dear friends graduated to Heaven several years ago. I miss them and their artistic inspiration and input into my life. We knew each other so well that both Marlo and Jill finished my sentences.

I enjoyed many friends over the years when I traveled to San Francisco, Hawaii, Colorado and back again to Washington. Over the years, a few of those loyal friends still called or e-mailed. Distance need not separate friends, but many long-distance friends seem to evaporate over time.

I guard my creative time in the art studio, but I make time for my special friends.

The beautiful earth
beneath my feet,
God planned it that way.

Mountains of grandeur,
oceans so deep,
majestic rain forest,
all silence me.

I watch you paint
in silent awe,
Creator, Designer
and
Soon Coming King.

I remember the day I heard this poem in my spirit. Friends invited us to spend a weekend at their condo on Schweitzer Mountain in Northern Idaho. Everyone else left for the day to ski. I looked out of the large living room window from high on the mountain. The skiers looked like tiny ants that moved across the snow. I felt incredulous at the view in front of me. As I stood there in awe of the enormous mountain, I heard the poem inside me. I only wrote what I heard without a single change. I always stand in awe of the Creator's canvases. The strength of His ocean, the power of His wind, and the beauty of His rain forest always leave me silently amazed. No one can capture beauty like God, the first artist.

I APPRECIATE THE TIME

I appreciate time
to create.

Time to ponder,
pray,
paint.

I appreciate every moment
every hour.

Destiny time,
knowing,
painting,
becoming time.

All that I am
in color, in line.

Before and after
becoming time.

I appreciate it all!

Time, that precious commodity, which never seems enough for all my projects and ideas over the course of a week. Experience taught me to guard my precious creative time. More and more things in this world steal our time. Some inventive people always come up with new talent robbers such as cell phones, apps that paint for you, or social media. I appreciate every silent hour in my art studio. To create effectively, artists need a lot of time to think and time to put those thoughts into artistic form. It takes time to hear and write a book, pen a poem, or compose an aria'. All artists I know struggle with the balance between life and time for art. When art defines our destiny, our passions need time set apart to develop and follow that destiny. Our creativity needs us to make it a priority and sustain it over the months and years. I try to accomplish something in art each day, even if I just organize my studio. I make my God-time priority, then my family, and then time for art. Between these daily personal goals, I also add indoor swimming, healthy meals, friends, and time to relax. All in all, these priorities add up to a busy day. As artists, we wear many hats and learn to adjust to variables and the unexpected needs and expectations of others. Sometimes I find myself a juggler with many distractions. Sometimes I just need to find a non-educational book and relax for the entire day.

Many artists I know do not possess an "off" button. Our creative lives exhilarate us, but also drain us. At the bottom line, I thank God for the time He gives me to create.

I AM AN EAGLE WITH WINGS

I do not paint
to sell.

I do not write
to publish.

Rather,
I write to write,
I paint to paint.

I am outside
the box!

I have always been
outside the box!

Inside would feel
strange.

I am not
a box person.

I am an eagle with wings!

In my art studio on a large piece of paper and in large black letters it says, "I have to paint and write for me." These two passions live within me and I remain incomplete unless I follow the road less traveled. I seek neither fame nor importance, but my passions energize me. My life outside the box frees me like nothing else. I never fit into the crowd. In fact, I dislike crowds. However, I like to sit on a bench or park lawn and watch the crowd pass me by. What I see around me in living color fascinates me. Poems write themselves when I watch the crowd. Always the quiet person in school, I never volunteered for any public speaking. Eagles possess a keen eye and see far into the distance. They fly when it becomes necessary to do so. I identify with a winged eagle. Always.

EARTH MUSIC

Earth music is how
each new generation
finds its own identity.

The old timers usually
never relate to the new timers.

New timers with new messages
and new hair styles.

Their earth music belongs
to them and only them.

It will fade away
when they fade away
and other new timers
will come up with
new earth music.

Music will always be new
because life is always new
and different.

Music defines each generation and blends diverse cultures. I grew up in the 60's, an era of change. We stepped outside the box in both dress and music. The Beatles album "Sgt. Pepper Lonely Hearts Club Band" lead the charge. The "Jefferson Airplane" flew overhead and the "Loving Spoonful" gave us soul food. The "white rabbit" disappeared into smoke and Elvis Presley induced every young girl to scream and dream of being his girl. Many, like myself, went to San Francisco and wore some flowers in our hair. The flower child generation wanted freedom like never before—the new timers with new messages and new hair styles. The years passed, and another generation replaced us. New earth music appeared on the horizon and a new generation emerged. The children of the 60's, now the older generation, find no identity with present music. The new timers also grow older and in time their music fades from the land because one generation moves on and makes room for the next. When I listen to the Beatles or Jefferson Airplane music, good memories return to this Baby Boomer. Earth music always brings memories, both good and bad, though music changes, it never fades from our minds. Earth music defines each generation.

GOD AND GOD, ALONE

The business of man
amazes me.

We busy ourselves
gathering,
storing,
building,
and
having.

For what?
What do we gain?

We all have this drive
to attain.

We are never satisfied.
Never.

The only thing of lasting value
most people never have.

God and God alone!

Life seems to fill up with things we own. We focus on the temporal world to make us happy and feel important. The world offers many new toys to satisfy our souls. Yet we never seem to find satisfaction with possessions. We always want more. I too fit into that category of dissatisfaction and the need to buy more. At the end of life, I will need to downsize, pass my things to family and grandchildren, and move into an assisted care facility. So, in the end, we lose all we gathered. In time, each of us fits into this category. We need to ask ourselves where our focus lies. On ourselves and our stuff? On God and our relationship with Him? At the end of our life, will we find ourselves in spiritual poverty and lack spiritual insight? We may find that whatever held importance, loses importance and holds no value to God. Our treasures in heaven increase by prayer and the things of God rather than on empty, meaningless temporal things that never make it to Heaven. No one takes their money to Heaven, not even a dime. So, let's put value on eternal things like prayer, a transparent relationship with the Creator, and on time to read His "instruction manual," the Bible. Heaven holds treasures of great worth.

THE TALL ONES

The tall ones
stand over us,
sentinels of time.

Listening,
guarding,
and protecting.

Nature's tall ones
came before us
and they will
be here
long after
we depart.

The tall ones
stand over us,
sentinels of time.

The "tall ones" of nature look down on our tiny world—the heavens, the clouds, and even the trees over us. Nature speaks without words and looks down over all creation. I think someday all will hear nature's voice. Children hear trees talk and heaven sing because they live uninhibited by adult thought and reason. The child inside me hears the trees talk and heaven sing. An artist and a writer see and hears different tones and colors. I hear with my spirit things others miss. When, near a mountain stream, I hear a poem and know the stream speaks it to me. But people wonder about you when you say things like, "I hear the stream speak to me." Therefore, I resist saying anything to anyone about the stream and forest's talk to me. But, I don't just imagine their voices, I hear them in my spirit.

A MARLO POEM

The painter Marlo
is a wonderful friend.

She understands my
need to paint
long into the
starry night
because she also paints
until the morning light.

Artists understand artists.

We will never paint
like each other
because we are artists
with our own inner vision.

The painter Marlo
will always be
my best friend
because
artists understand artists
always.

Marlo, my friend lives in Heaven. She graduated five years ago. I imagine she lives in a beautiful mansion with birds everywhere and paints every day in her awesome studio and art gallery just like she did here on the earth. She also writes poetry like she did here on the earth.

I remember the days we painted and laughed together. Marlo helped me see art with new eyes. She taught school for several years and I attended her art class once. She mesmerized all her students with her words. She knows art and she knows the history of each artist. When she drew a picture of the artist we got it. We really got it. I do not know another artist like my friend Marlo. She lived in the San Francisco Bay area and loved it there. She lived with such a free spirit and that city fit her personality. She loved life and I feel so blessed by her friendship. As singles, we enjoyed the opportunity to spend so much time together to discuss our passion—art. Her love for painting equals my love for painting. We shared so many things together. I own her best painting, "The Nude," truly a masterpiece. I feel so honored to hang it in our home. Someday, when we both reside in Heaven, I can't imagine the worth of that painting on earth. I feel sad she will not get to enjoy that success. Artists seldom live long enough to see the worth of their talent and passions.

ART ON THE GREEN AND JUNK ON THE LAWN

There is a very prestigious
art fair in my town called
Art on the Green.

My artist friends
had their own fair
across the street.

They showed their work
and called it
Junk on the Lawn.

I laughed
until my sides hurt
when I heard
their title.

Artists laugh a lot
at the absurdities of life.

"Art on the Green," a prestigious art venue in Coeur d' Alene, Idaho, boasts of a juried show. Those who do not make the grade are not allowed to show in the park. The committee rejected some very fine artist friends who decided to put up their own show on a neighborhood lawn and called it, "Junk on the Lawn." I laughed hysterically when I saw their sign. It provided a great statement about art and judging and who is in and who is out. Not everyone who gets in, is who gets in, in the end. Van Gogh wasn't judged in an art show, but he ended up being one of the most important participants in the art world of all time. I find it interesting how society feels they know who is great or accepted and who is not. It amazes me who truly comes out great in the end.

POEMS LIVE

Poems live far beyond
the life of the poet.

They live within,
they live without,
they live long,
and they live loud.

Poems belong to,
the creator who created them,
the listener who heard them
and the writer who wrote them.

Poems come to visit
and they stay as long
as we will listen to them.

Poems are snowflakes
and no snowflake
is the same in design.

I know because I love snow
I know because I love poems.

I know because I am a poet.

Poems belong to the poet until we pen them. Then they belong to the entire world. They last forever and endure long after the poet departs. Poems, like the finger of God, write themselves upon our hearts and travel with us wherever we go. Poems belong to the listener who hears them and embraces the message they speak. They speak a novel in a sentence and a revelation in a word. Short, powerful, and impacting, they paint in word form. When I finish a painting, I usually hear its poem. The correlation between paintings and their poems always fascinates me. I wish all painters before me had listened and written the poem that accompanied their painting. I now understand that poems live in the divine atmosphere that surrounds us. We need to stop and listen. The person who takes time to listen to the silence will hear them. It takes no special gift to hear the poem, rather the silent observer captures the moment and pens the poem. So, listen.

Writing at midnight
inspires me.

A small glass of wine
and an ocean of words.

Words flow onto paper
like breath from a baby.

I hear them,
I feel them,
I embrace them.

Words with impact,
emotion,
drama.

Midnight words
inspire me.

I hear poems. They come at morning, noon, evening, and in the midnight hours. They do not limit themselves to a specific time or place. When I hear them, I know it. They live inside me and through a myriad of ways they enter my mind and thoughts. I seldom change the words I hear inside. They seem perfect the way they come. Why change perfect? Poems speak my soul language and my paintings flow in color from within. In the silence of the midnight hour I hear many poems. No immediate needs distract me in the evening hours. When younger I spent more hours painting or writing at midnight. As I age, I find my resilience to stay up late wains. Near age 70 my creativity flows best during the daylight hours. Age overshadows my youth on the physical canvas of my body. I miss the "moon in the sky" inspirational hours. However, I find an ocean of words that wait for me in the morning.

WE ARE STILL CHILDREN INSIDE

Age is a number,
not a reality.

We are still children
inside.

Children again and again.

We see differently
because we see from within.

Aging comes with age.

Understanding comes with understanding,
and wisdom comes from within.

We are still children inside
no matter what age
we are outside.

This past year I turned seventy years old (young). As I age, the artist inside me retains the heart of a child. My pen brings out that small child. I'm still the tomboy who loves to walk in the woods, watch trains pass by, and sit by a quiet stream, I still daydream. So many memories stay with me of life on our land when we built a 2,200-square foot log home. I still enjoy wonderful memories of watching our children grow up and now our grandchildren. I keep the fire inside alive by painting and writing each day. The challenge of aging becomes part of my life. People grow old emotionally because they quit imparting their special God-given gift to the world around them. They lose the zing in life. They simply grow old and die with no goals, no energy, no new ideas, only old ones, and no dreams. Dreams keep us going. Dreams become goals in color. When we lose color, we die. Without color, we lose the will to live. Keep the color and keep the child alive inside of you.

THE GARDEN ANGEL

The garden angel
lives at the Bakken house.

She adores the artist
who lives inside the house.

She is the quiet majestic angel
who guards the artist.

She whispers prayers
from the earth into the heavens.

Her day is filled with quiet prayers
for the artist.

The months linger into years
and her prayers go on and on and on.

When the artist works in her garden
she winks at her now and then.

The garden angel loves
the artist who owns the
beautiful majestic garden.

She whispers prayers
from the earth into the heavens
and her prayers go on and on and on.

My special artist friend owns a metal piece of art work called "Garden Angel," who lives in her inspiring garden. The metal piece caught my eye on a day when I photographed her home, studio, and garden. The poem whispered itself in my ear as I photographed it in the soft winter snow. The silent angel seemed to whisper to me, "I love my special friend, the artist who lives and creates here." The sculpture piece seemed to come alive that peaceful cold winter day. I believe we all possess an angel who watches, guards, and loves each person from birth. The heart of the Creator sent angels to walk with each of us day by day until we can walk no more. Then we walk in the light with Him in heaven or without him in the darkness of hell. God does not violate our ability to choose. Hopefully we make the right choice.

The poems live here
like the mist across the lake.

I come here often
to pen a few more poems,
a few more memories.

The quiet lake
has captured my heart
and my pen.

Yes, it can be stormy
but it can also be
quiet and serene.

I come here often
to catch a few more poems
drifting across the lake.

I close my eyes and see the beautiful lake. The poems live at this lake and wait for me to catch them in the summer morning breeze. The long lake often grows very tumultuous. Storms come upon the lake suddenly and disappear just as suddenly. My family and I camped here many times in the summer months.

In my junior high school years, my parents bought property on a lake near Tacoma WA. We spent weekend's water skiing, swimming with friends, and telling scary stories around the campfire late at night. I always loved rivers, lakes, and anything to do with water. In my fondest childhood memory, I sit on a very large bolder surrounded by the river. My father fishes up and down the creek, and I listen to the sounds of nature around me.

Our family camped at Priest Lake for many years. The poems drifted to me from across the deep blue waters. The stormy weather always proved awesome and the poems wrote themselves in the intense raging winds. Storms came over the mountains and raced full tilt at Indian Creek Camp Ground. When we saw a storm come down the lake we raced for safety because it came like a speeding train toward our tent or camper. Peaceful, serene, and warm days also came when soft spoken poems drifted across the cool water into my pocket. Priest Lake etched itself across my soul and remains a beautiful painting etched on the walls of my heart. My eyes may grow dim in the winter of life, but the inner vision of this lake never fades.

THE STUDIO

The studio is quiet
and I am quiet.

Waiting for the inspiration
and the journey to begin.

Where will we travel
what shall we see?

How far will we go
and what treasure
will we find?

How will it end
and what will be
the outcome?

Will it be accepted
and will it be seen?

The studio awaits me.

My art studio forms a world within a world. Full of activity and quiet at the same time, it energizes my think tank. I come here to think and to express what I think. It connects my world with my best friend, the Creator, who sits beside me. We are best friends. My studio remains quiet. Paintings thumb tacked on the walls and posters of other artists I admire cover the slanted ceiling. The room feels crowded with my closest friends. The hours spent in creativity seem like minutes. I lose track of time and the world in which I live. This creative world remains void of time. Boredom finds no place here. Boredom comes for people without direction or vision. I possess both. To where will this volume of creative work journey and who will view it? The sands of time answer that question.

ETERNITY DRAWS NEAR EVERY SECOND

Eternity is a place,
a very important place.

It is coming at you
second by second.

You cannot
ignore it,
avoid it,
deny it.

We are all going there
someday.

It is your choice,
for better or for worse,
so, choose wisely.

Choose very, very wisely!

Eternity
is
coming
at you
now!

Heaven and hell exist in real places even if we choose not to believe in them. The Creator of the universe says they exist. The Creator (God–Jesus–Holy Spirit) presents Himself to us many times throughout our lives. We get to choose to ignore, avoid, or deny Him. He gives us the chance to confess our sins to Jesus and accept His love and grace. Then we will spend Eternity with our Creator. God made a way back to Himself through the death of His Son Jesus. No other way exists regardless of what other people tell us. Our choice determines our eternal dwelling place. One place burns hotter than the sun and the other place gives us peace and rest forever. So, choose wisely. Choose very wisely. I want to see you in heaven where we will rejoice together. Maybe we will even write some poetry or do a painting together. I pray for your choice.

INDEX OF TITLES

TM

END OF THE BOOK NOTES BY AUTHOR

I want to thank you for reading this book, "The Dreamer." I hope these poems touched your heart and soul. In some small way, I hope you saw and heard the quiet voice of God through these pages. I hear poems and I write what I hear. The voice is the "I Am" God of Creation. I greet Him every morning and the One to whom I say, "thank you" before I go to sleep. He is the Lord of lords, the lover of my soul and my closest companion in my walk here on this earth.

I encourage you to pursue your passions and follow your dreams in whatever art form suites you best. God bless as you travel on your earthly journey.

Paintings may be viewed on my website: *www.karenhol.com*

c 2017 By Karen Hol
Published by
A division of To God Be the Glory
Spokane, WA